21st Century
Basic Skills
Library

WHAT DO ANIMALS DO IN WINTER?

by Rebecca Felix

Cherry Lake Publishing • Ann Arbor, Michigan

1

Published in the United States of America
by Cherry Lake Publishing
Ann Arbor, Michigan
www.cherrylakepublishing.com

Consultant: Marla Conn, ReadAbility, Inc.
Editorial direction and book production: Red Line Editorial

Photo Credits: Menno Schaefer/Shutterstock Images, cover, 1; urbanlight/
Shutterstock Images, 4; Kenneth Keifer/Shutterstock Images, 6; Tom
Grundy/Shutterstock Images, 8; Scott Leslie/Minden Pictures/Corbis, 10;
erniedecker/iStock/Thinkstock, 12; RCKeller/iStockphoto/Thinkstock, 14;
Scott E Read/Shutterstock Images, 16; outdoorsman/Shutterstock Images,
18; Andrew Koturanov/Shutterstock Images, 20

Library of Congress Cataloging-in-Publication Data
Felix, Rebecca, 1984- author.
  What do animals do in winter? / by Rebecca Felix.
     pages cm. -- (Let's look at winter)
  Audience: Age 6.
  Audience: Grades K to 3.
  Includes index.
  ISBN 978-1-63137-607-8 (hardcover) -- ISBN 978-1-63137-652-8 (pbk.) --
  ISBN 978-1-63137-697-9 (pdf ebook) -- ISBN 978-1-63137-742-6 (ebook)
 1. Animals--Wintering--Juvenile literature. I. Title.
  QL753.F46 2013
  591.4'3--dc23
                                        2014004564

Cherry Lake Publishing would like to acknowledge the work of The
Partnership for 21st Century Skills. Please visit www.p21.org for more
information.

Printed in the United States of America
Corporate Graphics Inc.
July 2014

TABLE OF CONTENTS

Cold

Winter is cold. Many plants die. There is less food for animals.

What kind of animal is this?

Animals **sense** these changes. Their **behavior** also changes.

Rest

Some animals **hibernate**.
Many bats sleep all winter.

What Do You See?

This turtle is underwater. How can you tell?

Some turtles rest in deep mud underwater all winter.

What Do You See?

Geese migrate. How many geese do you see?

Birds

Many birds **migrate**. They fly to warmer places. They find food there.

Some birds grow more feathers. This helps them keep warm.

Fur

Some animals grow thicker fur to keep warm. Red foxes do this.

Arctic foxes turn white for winter. White fur helps the fox hide in snow.

Soon, snow melts. Spring arrives. What do animals do in spring?

Find Out More

BOOK

Kosara, Tori. *Hibernation*. New York: Scholastic, 2011.

WEB SITE

Animals in Winter—Kidz Club

*www.kizclub.com/storytime/winteranimals/winteranimals.
  html*

Read or listen to an e-book about animals in winter.

Glossary

behavior (be-HAYV-yur) the way an animal acts

hibernate (HYE-bur-nate) to go into a deep, long sleep
  during winter

migrate (MYE-grate) to move to another place

sense (SENS) to be aware of something

Home and School Connection

Use this list of words from the book to help your child become a better reader. Word games and writing activities can help beginning readers reinforce literacy skills.

animals	fly	melts	soon
arctic foxes	food	migrate	spring
arrives	fur	more	tell
bats	geese	mud	thicker
behavior	grow	places	turn
birds	helps	plants	turtles
changes	hibernate	red foxes	underwater
deep	hide	rest	warm
die	keep	sense	warmer
feathers	less	sleep	white
find	many	snow	winter

What Do You See?

What Do You See? is a feature paired with select photos in this book. It encourages young readers to interact with visual images in order to build the ability to integrate content in various media formats.

You can help your child further evaluate photos in this book with additional activities. Look at the images in the book without the What Do You See? feature. Ask your child to describe one detail in each image, such as a food, activity, or setting.

Index

About the Author

Rebecca Felix is an editor and writer from Minnesota. It gets very cold there in winter. Geese in Minnesota migrate south in winter. Deer that live there grow thicker fur.